THIS NOTEBOOKS BELONGS TO:

Made in the USA
Monee, IL
14 January 2023

25252634R00083